DINOSAUR WORLD

T. rex

The Adventure of Tyrannosaurus rex

Written by Michael Dahl

Illustrated by Jeff Yesh

Thanks to our advisers for their expertise, research, knowledge, and advice:

Brent H. Breithaupt, Director
Geological Museum, University of Wyoming
Laramie, Wyoming

Peter Dodson, Ph.D.
Professor of Earth and Environmental Sciences
University of Pennsylvania
Philadelphia, Pennsylvania

Susan Kesselring, M.A.
Literacy Educator
Rosemount-Apple Valley-Eagan (Minnesota) School District

PICTURE WINDOW BOOKS
Minneapolis, Minnesota

Managing Editor: Bob Temple
Creative Director: Terri Foley
Editors: Nadia Higgins, Brenda Haugen
Editorial Adviser: Andrea Cascardi
Copy Editor: Laurie Kahn
Designer: Nathan Gassman
Page production: Picture Window Books
The illustrations in this book were rendered digitally.

Picture Window Books
5115 Excelsior Boulevard
Suite 232
Minneapolis, MN 55416
1-877-845-8392
www.picturewindowbooks.com

Printed in the United States of America.

Library of Congress Cataloging-in-Publication Data
Dahl, Michael.
T. rex : the adventure of tyrannosaurus rex / written by
Michael Dahl ; illustrated by Jeff Yesh.
p. cm. — (Dinosaur world)
Includes bibliographical references and index.
Summary: Explains how scientists learn about dinosaurs and
what their discoveries have revealed about Tyrannosaurus rex.
ISBN 1-4048-0139-1
1. Tyrannosaurus rex Juvenile literature. [1. Tyrannosaurus
rex. 2. Dinosaurs.] I. Yesh, Jeff, 1971- ill. II. Title.
QE862.S3 D35 2004
567.912'9—dc21
                                    2003004152

No humans lived during the time of the dinosaurs. No people heard them roar, saw their scales, or felt their feathers.

The giant creatures are gone, but their fossils, or remains, lie hidden in the earth. Dinosaur skulls, skeletons, and eggs have been buried in rock for millions of years.

All around the world, scientists dig up fossils and carefully study them. Bones show how tall the dinosaurs stood. Claws and teeth show how they grabbed and what they ate. Scientists compare fossils with the bodies of living creatures such as birds and reptiles, who are relatives of the dinosaurs. Every year, scientists learn more and more about the giants that have disappeared.

Studying fossils and figuring out how dinosaurs lived is like putting together the pieces of a puzzle that is millions of years old.

This is what some of those pieces can tell us about the dinosaur known as Tyrannosaurus rex.

A summer breeze swept through the forest. Pine trees rustled softly.
Tyrannosaurus rex (tuh-RAN-uh-SAWR-us REKS) sniffed the air and stretched his jaws.

The dinosaur stopped by a muddy stream. Farther up the stream, Edmontosaurus (ed-MON-tuh-SAWR-us), a gentle plant-eater, grazed on moss growing on the banks.

Tyrannosaurus rex sniffed again. He caught the scent of his next prey.

5

6

Tyrannosaurus rex, or T. rex, was one of the most ferocious meat-eating dinosaurs. *Tyrannosaurus* means "tyrant lizard." A tyrant is a cruel, powerful ruler. *Rex* means "king."

T. rex grew as long as a city bus and as tall as an elephant.

As Tyrannosaurus rex smelled Edmontosaurus, he snapped his jaws open and shut. T. rex had a mouthful of curving teeth as long as dinner knives. Most of the teeth had jagged, saw-like edges. They could slice through dinosaur skin and crush bone.

Tyrannosaurus had some of the largest, strongest neck muscles of any carnivore. The muscles helped him tear off huge chunks of meat. Tyrannosaurus could bite off an Edmontosaurus leg with a single, deadly snap.

Scientists have found some T. rex jaws with more than 60 teeth. That means the dinosaur had twice as many teeth as a human.

Tyrannosaurus rex followed the scent of his prey. He marched upstream, stomping through the muddy water. Each mighty step carried him 15 feet (4½ meters) closer to his victim.

T. rex's three large toes each carried a sharp claw. The claws would help him grip his victim as T. rex's ferocious teeth tore at the hide.

Tyrannosaurus rex sniffed the air again. He smelled something new. Another Edmontosaurus was roaming nearby. This new dinosaur was quietly feeding along the riverbank.

T. rex had an extra-powerful sense of smell. He could sniff out living and dead animals. If no fresh meat was close by, T. rex would scavenge, feeding on creatures that already were dead.

Tyrannosaurus rex turned, and his mighty tail swung around.
It whipped through a cloud of dragonflies darting above the water.

When the predator was running, the stiff, pointed tail helped him keep his balance as he made fast turns.

T. rex's tail was made up of dozens of bones. Many of T. rex's bones were hollow, like a bird's. The light bones helped the giant creature run quickly after prey.

Tyrannosaurus rex soon saw the second Edmontosaurus. The plant-eater was grazing on ferns with his back to the deadly predator. T. rex would be able to reach his victim in only a few quick steps.

Tyrannosaurus rex had eyes the size of grapefruits. The eyes were pointed forward. This helped the carnivore judge how far he would have to run in order to reach his prey.

Tyrannosaurus rex pounced on the plant-eater. Razor-sharp teeth sank into the creature's chunky back. Edmontosaurus roared with pain.

The plant eater turned, whipping his tail at T. rex. Snap! Tyrannosaurus rex jerked his powerful neck and caught the plant-eater's tail in his curving teeth.

T. rex's arms were useless in a fight because they were so short. The dinosaur probably used his arms to hold up his body when he leaned down to eat his prey.

Another mighty roar shook the forest. The Edmontosaurus
from the muddy stream had come looking for her companion.
When she saw the ferocious T. rex, she bellowed loud and long.

T. rex whipped his head to stare at the second dinosaur.
As T. rex turned, he lost hold of the tail between his teeth.
A long, bloody wound tore through his victim's tail.

Both Edmontosauruses staggered through the forest. T. rex raced after them. One of the plant-eaters soon would become Tyrannosaurus rex's next meal.

Tyrannosaurus: Where ...

Tyrannosaurus rex has been discovered mostly in North America: Colorado, North Dakota, South Dakota, Montana, Texas, Wyoming, New Mexico, and Saskatchewan.

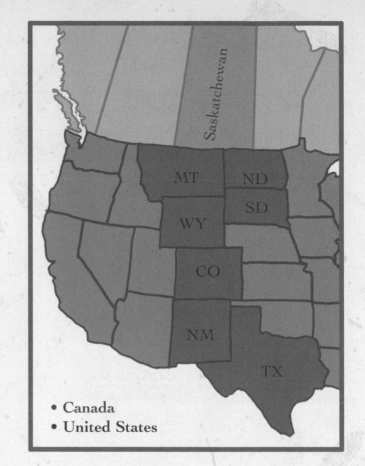

- Canada
- United States

... and When

The "Age of Dinosaurs" began 248 million years ago (mya). If we imagine the time from the beginning of the dinosaur age to the present as one day, dinosaurs lived almost 18 hours—and humans appeared just 10 minutes ago!

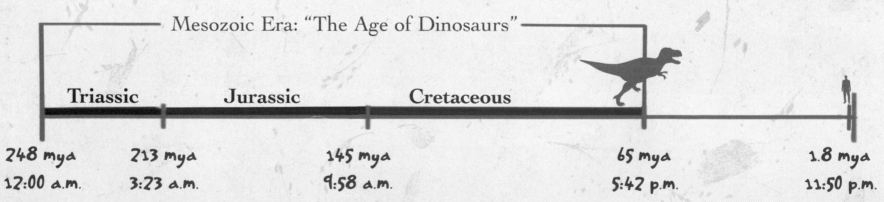

Mesozoic Era: "The Age of Dinosaurs"

Triassic	Jurassic	Cretaceous	
248 mya	213 mya	145 mya	65 mya	1.8 mya
12:00 a.m.	3:23 a.m.	9:58 a.m.	5:42 p.m.	11:50 p.m.

Triassic—Dinosaurs first appear. Early mammals appear.
Jurassic—First birds appear.
Cretaceous—Flowering plants appear. By the end of this era, all dinosaurs disappear.

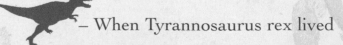

— When Tyrannosaurus rex lived

— First humans appear

Digging Deeper

No Longer King

Tyrannosaurus rex once was thought to be the largest carnivorous dinosaur that ever lived. In 1993, scientists found bones of an even larger meat-eating dinosaur. The new creature was named Giganotosaurus (JYE-gah-NO-toe-SAWR-us). T. rex still is considered one of the fiercest carnivores from the Age of Dinosaurs.

Cannibals

T. rexes may have fought among themselves, sometimes eating one another after a kill. Scientists have discovered T. rex fossils with T. rex bite marks on them. They also have found bones of Tyrannosaurus rex inside the stomach of another T. rex.

Dino Droppings

Scientists closely study many kinds of fossils, including coprolites, or dinosaur droppings. Coprolites can show what T. rex ate. Inside one dropping, as big as a football, were Edmontosaurus bones. Inside another rested the bony collar of a Triceratops (try-SEHR-uh-tops).

Powerful Push-ups

Scientists recently have discovered that T. rex's little arms had powerful muscles. T. rex may have used its arms to help push itself up from the ground after sleeping.

Words to Know

carnivore—a meat-eating animal

dinosaur—a land reptile that lived in prehistoric times. All dinosaurs died out millions of years ago.

fossil—the remains of a plant or animal that lived between thousands and millions of years ago

moss—a soft, clumpy plant that usually grows in swamps and wetlands

scavenge—to feed on an animal that's already dead

predator—an animal that hunts and eats other animals

prey—an animal that is hunted and eaten by other animals

To Learn More

At the Library

Cohen, Daniel. *Tyrannosaurus rex.* Mankato, Minn.: Bridgestone Books, 2001.

Landau, Elaine. *Tyrannosaurus rex.* New York: Children's Press, 1999.

Relf, Patricia. *A Dinosaur Named Sue: The Story of the Colossal Fossil: The World's Most Complete T. rex.* New York: Scholastic, 2000.

Zoehfeld, Kathleen Weidner. *Terrible Tyrannosaurs.* New York: HarperCollins Publishers, 2001.

On the Web

Enchanted Learning: Zoom Dinosaurs
http://www.EnchantedLearning.com/subjects/dinosaurs
For information, games, and jokes about dinosaurs, fossils, and prehistoric life

The Natural History Museum, London: Dino Directory
http://flood.nhm.ac.uk/cgi-bin/dino
For an alphabetical database of information on the Age of Dinosaurs

University of California, Berkeley: Museum of Paleontology
http://www.ucmp.berkeley.edu/museum/k-12.html
On-line exhibits, articles, activities, and resources for teachers and students

Fact Hound
Fact Hound offers a safe, fun way to find Web sites related to this book. All of the sites on Fact Hound have been researched by our staff.
http://www.facthound.com

1. Visit the Fact Hound home page.
2. Enter a search word related to this book, or type in this special code: 1404801391.
3. Click on the FETCH IT button.

Your trusty Fact Hound will fetch the best sites for you!